# HANGZHOU TRAVEL GUIDE 2024

*A Voyage through History, Culture, and Culinary Delights*

**Michelle Strauss**

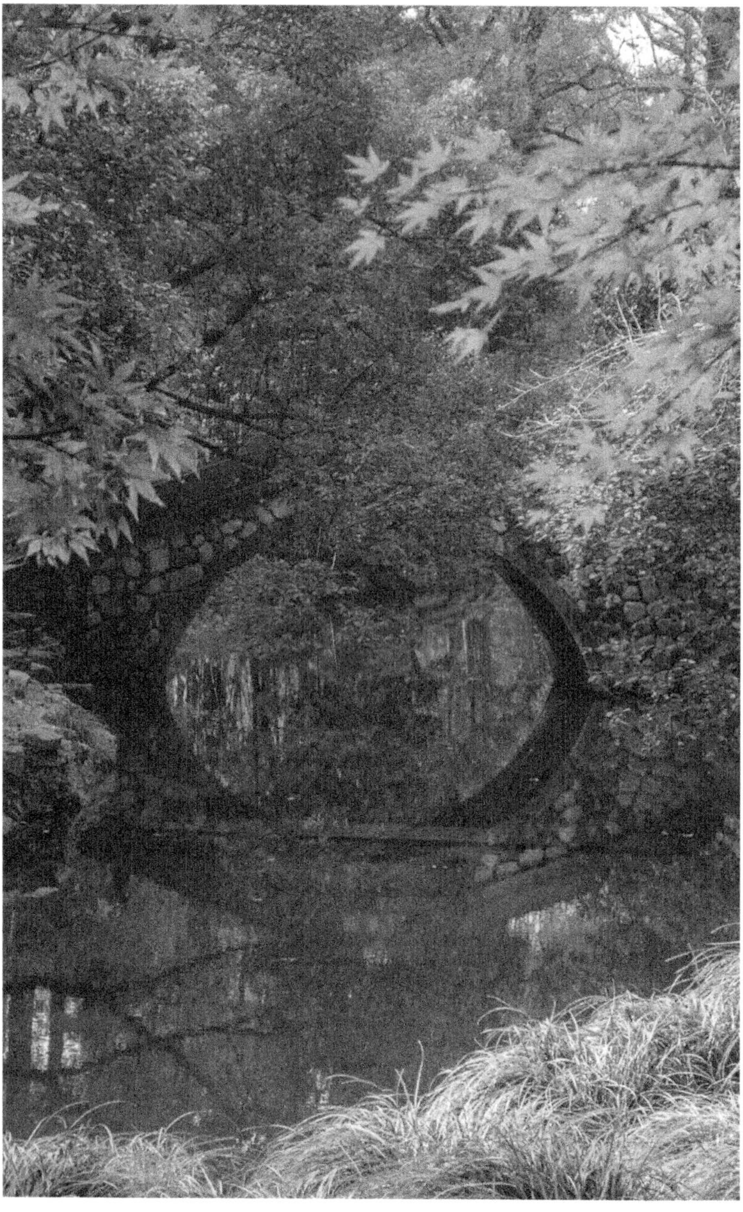

Copyright © 2023 by Michelle Strauss

All rights reserved. No part of this book may be reproduced, stored in a retrieval system, or transmitted in any form or by any means, electronic, mechanical, photocopying, recording, scanning, or otherwise, without the prior written permission of the publisher, except for brief quotations embodied in critical reviews and certain other non-commercial uses permitted by copyright law.

# Disclaimer

This travel guide is provided for general informational purposes only. The publishers and authors have compiled the content of this guide with care and to the best of their knowledge at the time of publication. However, the travel industry is dynamic, and services, sites, and amenities can change before the next edition.

Information regarding travel regulations, visa policies, health and safety guidelines, transportation schedules, and accommodation details are subject to change without notice. The publishers and authors cannot accept responsibility for any inconvenience, loss, or damage that may occur as a result of relying on the information provided in this guide.

Readers are strongly encouraged to verify any critical information directly from official sources, such as embassies, consulates, tourist boards, and service providers, before making travel plans. Additionally, the publishers and authors do not endorse or guarantee the services mentioned within the guide. Opinions expressed are those of the individual contributors and do not necessarily reflect those of the publishers.

The inclusion of establishments, locales, or services does not constitute an endorsement of quality, service, or value, and no payment has been received for their inclusion. The publishers and authors accept no responsibility for the quality of goods or services listed in this guide.

Maps and travel route suggestions are intended as an aid to help you enjoy your travels. They should not be used as the sole means of navigation. Always carry official maps and consult local authorities or guides when necessary.

By using this guide, you acknowledge that you are doing so at your own risk and have chosen to do so freely. You agree not to hold the publishers, authors, or any associated persons or entities liable for any outcomes of your travels in Penang or for the reliance on any information contained herein.

Please travel responsibly and respect the customs, traditions, and laws of Penang and Malaysia. Enjoy your journey!

# BONUS PAGES

- Helpful Phrase Guide
- Shopping Guide
- Restaurant Guide
- Local Recipes
- Sample Itineraries
- Travel Journal
- Maps and Location

Scan to Access Hangzhou Railway Station

Scan code to Access HANGZHOU From Airport

## About the Author

Michelle Strauss is a seasoned travel guide expert with a passion for exploring the world's diverse destinations. With years of experience in the travel industry, she has become a trusted source of knowledge and inspiration for adventurers and explorers alike.

Michelle's journey in travel began at a young age when she embarked on a cross-country road trip with her family, igniting her lifelong fascination with discovering new places and cultures. Her insatiable curiosity led her to explore remote corners of the globe, from the bustling markets of Marrakech to the tranquil temples of Kyoto.

Throughout her extensive travels, Michelle developed a keen eye for uncovering hidden gems, navigating foreign landscapes, and immersing herself in local cultures. Her commitment to responsible travel and sustainable practices has not only enriched her own experiences but also positively impacted the communities she has visited.

As a travel guide expert, Michelle Strauss has dedicated herself to sharing her insights and expertise with fellow travelers, helping them create unforgettable journeys of their own. Her writing captures the essence of each destination, providing practical tips, cultural context, and personal anecdotes that inspire and inform.

When she's not on the road, Michelle enjoys researching and curating travel content, delving into the histories and traditions of the places she visits, and honing her culinary skills by recreating recipes from around the world. Her goal is to empower travelers to explore with confidence and respect, fostering a deeper connection between people and the planet.

# Discover Hangzhou

INTRODUCTION ............................................................... 11

    History of Hangzhou ..................................................... 12

    Climate and Geography ................................................ 14

    Best Time to Visit ......................................................... 14

2. Getting to Hangzhou and Around ..................................... 17

    Via Air .......................................................................... 17

    Via Train ...................................................................... 18

    By Road ....................................................................... 18

    Local Transport ........................................................... 19

3. Accommodations ............................................................. 21

4. Dining and Cuisine in Hangzhou ...................................... 25

5. Hangzhou Attractions and Activities ................................ 29

6. Culture and Festival ......................................................... 35

7. Useful Travelers Information ............................................ 41

8. Itineraries and Guided Tours ........................................... 47

APPENDICES ................................................................. 51

Calendar of Events for the Year ............................................. 55

Bonus Chapters .............................................................. 61

    Phrasebook Guide ...................................................... 61

Sample Itineraries .......................................................... 63

    Family-Friendly Adventure Itinerary .................................... 63

    Solo Travelers Itinerary ............................................... 64

    Romantic Adventure Itinerary ........................................... 65

    Culinary Adventure Itinerary ........................................... 66

Hangzhou Restaurant Guide with Local Recipes ................................ 69

Hangzhou Shopping Guide for Visitors ........................................ 73

## INTRODUCTION

While sipping my freshly prepared jasmine tea, the calm waters of West Lake were illuminated by the golden glow of the early sun. The perfume blended with the fragrance of lotuses in bloom, giving me the impression that Hangzhou was personally greeting me.

It was my first morning in this city, where every stone walk has a tale to tell and where history echoes from the willow-lined banks. I came here looking for a fusion of the old and the new, and even in these peaceful hours, I could hear the city rising. The day ahead would provide strolls through vibrant marketplaces, a leisurely boat ride across the lake, and a trip through winding lanes that led to magnificent temples. The thought of all the stories I would hear, the food I would sample, and the sights that might inspire my own Hangzhou narrative made my heart accelerate.

This journey was more than simply another location on a map; it was an attempt to establish a closer relationship with a culture that had long captivated me virtually. I was eager to include myself in this fascinating city's colorful tapestry with each step.

## History of Hangzhou

The name "Heaven on Earth" was coined to describe Hangzhou, the capital of Zhejiang province in China, because of its captivating natural surroundings and rich cultural legacy. It is a city where contemporary architecture and traditional Chinese poetry coexist together, resulting in an ambiance that is at once vividly modern and evocatively old.

The city is centered on the famous West Lake, a UNESCO World Heritage site surrounded by lush hills and well-planned gardens that have served as an inspiration to poets and painters for generations.

In addition to being a popular travel destination, Hangzhou is home to many IT giants and startups, serving as a center for innovation and technology.

Hangzhou's history dates back to than 2,200 years, during which it served as the Grand Canal's southernmost point. During the 12th and 13th centuries, it prospered as the capital of the Southern Song Dynasty, becoming a prominent center of politics and culture. It is well known that Marco Polo called it the most magnificent city on Earth. Despite dynasty shifts, wars, and revolutions, Hangzhou has managed to hold onto its significance and historical landmarks, such as the Lingyin Temple and the Six Harmonies Pagoda, which stand as reminders of its colorful history.

## Climate and Geography

Hangzhou, which is surrounded by undulating hills and is at the southernmost point of the Yangtze River Delta, is distinguished by its flatlands and the West Lake region.

The city is traversed by the Qiantang River, which is well-known for its enormous tidal bore.

Four different seasons characterize the humid subtropical climate: warm and flowering springs, hot and humid summers, cold and harvest-rich autumns, and frigid, sometimes snowy winters.

## Best Time to Visit

The months of spring and fall are often the greatest times to visit Hangzhou.

**Spring (March through May):** This season is characterized by a slow increase in temperature, with averages between 10°C and 25°C (50°F and 77°F).

Hangzhou celebrates springtime with a flurry of flowers, particularly azaleas and cherry blossoms, which makes it a charming time of year to visit. The West Lake region is especially lovely when the surrounding vegetation blossoms. The weather is nice for outdoor activities, and there is a modest amount of tourist traffic.

**Autumn (September to November):** With mild, moderate temperatures between 15°C and 25°C (59°F and 77°F), autumn offers a break from the summer heat.

Autumn colors transform the surrounding vegetation into vibrant shades of orange and scarlet, creating a striking sight of the West Lake. The Mid-Autumn Festival is celebrated during this season as well, providing an opportunity to partake in mooncake tasting and learn about local customs.

In addition, spring and fall have the benefit of being outside summer's busiest travel seasons, which means fewer people and a more laid-back atmosphere. It's also a fantastic season for outdoor pursuits like leisurely boat rides on West Lake or hiking in the nearby hills.

# Click to Access **Hangzhou**

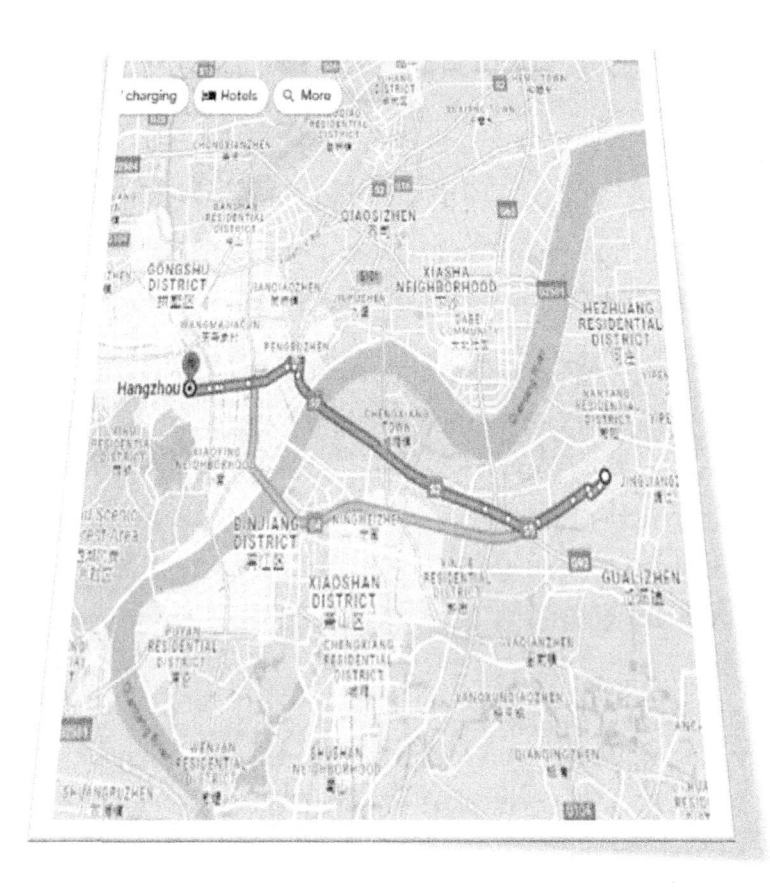

## 2. Getting to Hangzhou and Around

### Via Air

One of the main airports in the Yangtze River Delta region, Hangzhou Xiaoshan International Airport serves the city of Hangzhou. The airport serves a large number of international and domestic routes to locations in Asia, Europe, and North America, as well as linking Hangzhou to key cities around China. The city core is around 27 kilometers from the airport and may be reached by buses, taxis, or the Airport Express shuttle. There are stops at popular hotels and tourist destinations on the handy shuttle service.

**Via Train**

Because Hangzhou is a key railway hub in Eastern China, important cities like Shanghai, Beijing, Guangzhou, and Shenzhen can easily reach Hangzhou by high-speed train. There are many rail stations in the city, the biggest and most often utilized for long-distance travel being Hangzhou East Railway Station. Purchases of tickets may be made by automated machines at the stations, at ticket counters, or online. From Shanghai, high-speed trains may take as little as one hour to reach Hangzhou, providing a convenient and swift mode of transportation.

**By Road**

China's highway network connects Hangzhou to other major cities. Numerous bus terminals inside the city serve as departure and arrival points for long-distance buses that link it to other provincial towns and cities. There's also the option of driving to Hangzhou, which is made possible by the Hangzhou Bay Bridge and allows for a quicker trip from places like Ningbo. Although international visitors may hire a car, they should be aware that driving in China requires a Chinese driver's license.

## Local Transport

Once in Hangzhou, one may choose from a range of local transit choices:

**Public Buses:** The city's vast bus network provides an affordable means of transportation. However, if you don't know Mandarin, it might be packed and hard to get about.

**Subway:** The metro system in Hangzhou is growing quickly and offers a quick and easy method to go about the city. It links Hangzhou Railway Station, commercial areas, and popular tourist destinations.

**Taxis:** Taxis are widely available and may be booked via hotel concierges or hailed on the street. Applications for ridesharing are also quite popular and maybe a practical substitute.

**Bicycles and E-bikes:** There is a public bicycle rental program in Hangzhou, and there are bike lanes in many locations. Rentable e-bikes are another option for getting about the city, particularly in the West Lake area.

**Tourist Boats**: There are tourist boats that provide various itineraries around the picturesque areas of West Lake for people who like to explore the area.

Walking is a good alternative since a lot of Hangzhou's attractions are near to one another, especially around the West Lake region.

# 3. Accommodations

Hangzhou has a variety of lodging alternatives to suit all budgets and tastes, including traditional guesthouses that give a more genuine experience in addition to luxurious accommodations. Below is a thorough explanation of every category:

## Luxury Hotels

**Hangzhou Xanadu Resort:** Situated at 112 West Lake Avenue, this resort features a full-service spa, an indoor pool, and fine dining options in addition to its spectacular views of West Lake. Its rooms combine contemporary elegance with traditional Chinese design.

Located at 678 Shixin Road, the Grand Dynasty Hotel is renowned for its opulent design that pays homage to Hangzhou's former royal era. It has large rooms, a rooftop garden with views of the metropolitan skyline, and an executive lounge.

## Mid-range Hotels

The Jade Emperor Hotel is located at 157 Yugu Road, close to the botanical gardens. It has a restaurant providing both local and foreign food, a fitness facility, and cozy rooms with contemporary conveniences.

*Scan QR with your Device to Access Hotels*

Situated at 2 Huancheng West Road in Hangzhou, the Lakeview Hotel offers an ideal combination of luxury and convenience. Its well-appointed rooms provide stunning views of West Lake, and the main attractions are easily accessible by foot.

## Budget Options

**Hangzhou Serenity Hostel:** Located at 37 Nanshan Road, this hostel caters to budget-conscious tourists with simple, uncluttered rooms and dormitory-style lodging. Both West Lake and busy Qinghefang Street are not far away.

Located at 62-3 Nanshan Road, the Westlake Youth Hostel is a well-liked destination for travelers because of its welcoming ambiance, shared kitchen, and convenient proximity to nearby markets and public transit.

## Traditional Guesthouses

Nestled by the West Lake at 6 Qingnian Road, the Liuying Hotel is a guesthouse with traditional Chinese courtyard architecture, classical furniture, and peaceful grounds that evoke a sense of historical elegance.

Tea Boutique Hotel: This little guesthouse honors Hangzhou's tea culture and is situated at 124 Shuguang Road.

It offers visitors a peaceful haven with rooms decorated with tea themes and a charming tea house where they may partake in traditional tea rituals.

Every kind of lodging provides a distinctive experience catered to various tastes and price ranges, all the while giving guests access to Hangzhou's breathtaking scenery and diverse cultural offerings.

# 4. Dining and Cuisine in Hangzhou

## High-End Dining

The sophisticated dining scene in Hangzhou provides amazing culinary experiences, combining traditional Hangzhou cuisine—which is renowned for its subtle tastes and fresh ingredients—with an opulent setting.

Lou Wai Lou (楼外楼) - Location: Xihu District, Hangzhou, No. 30 Gushan Road. Located on the banks of West Lake, Lou Wai Lou is a landmark eatery that dates back to 1848. It is well-known for its traditional fare, which includes Beggar's Chicken and West Lake Fish in Sweet and Sour Sauce and is served in a classy atmosphere with views of the lake.

Four Seasons Hotel Hangzhou in West Lake, 5 Lingyin Road; Jin Sha (金沙). This superb Chinese restaurant, which has won many awards, specializes in Shanghainese, Cantonese, and regional Hangzhou dishes. The hotel's lagoon views and private dining rooms make it the ideal location for an opulent meal.

## Local Eats

Hangzhou has a wide variety of restaurants that provide well-known and traditional foods for visitors who want to fully experience the local cuisine.

Grandma's Home (碘婆家): spread around the city in various locales. Locals like this restaurant because it serves affordable home-style Zhejiang food, including stir-fried shrimp and dongpo pork.

Food Street He Dong Road is located at He Dong Road in the Xihu District. With its abundance of little restaurants and street sellers offering regional delicacies like Hangzhou Xiaolongbao (soup dumplings), Pian Er Chuan noodles, and Crispy Stinky Tofu, this lively food strip is a food lover's heaven.

Address: 83 Renhe Road, Shangcheng District Zhi Wei Guan (知味观). Zhi Wei Guan, a Hangzhou institution that opened in 1913, offers a range of classic Hangzhou meals and dim sum in a setting rich in culture and history.

## Street Food

For those who like to sample real local food, Hangzhou offers a diverse array of fast snacks and traditional tastes in its street food scene.

Known for its traditional delicacies, Qinghefang Ancient Street is situated in the ancient neighborhood. Favorite dishes from the area include Crispy Fried Squid, Hangzhou-style Baozi, and Dragon Whiskers Candy.

**Hefang Street Food Market**: This lively location offers a wide range of street food treats, including mung bean cakes, sticky rice balls in fermented rice wine, and Ningbo Tangyuan, a kind of sweet soup dumpling.

## Special Diets and Vegetarian

Hangzhou has a range of selections to suit various dietary restrictions, making it a great choice for vegetarians and people following special diets.

> The address of Vegetarian House (素食之家) is 83 Longjing Road. This restaurant serves a wide variety of vegetarian meals made with tofu, mushrooms, and other plant-based components that resemble the tastes and textures of classic Chinese animal dishes.
>
> The local location of the worldwide chain Loving Hut is located at 147 Nanshan Road. From Chinese-style stir-fries to vegan sweets from the West, Loving Hut offers a broad variety of vegan cuisine.
>
> Soul Kitchen is a contemporary café with an emphasis on organic, vegetarian-friendly, and healthful food located at 1 Baishaquan, Shuguang Road. They cater to health-conscious guests by providing a range of vegan and gluten-free alternatives.

These places are renowned for their ability to accommodate specific diets without sacrificing the depth of Hangzhou's culinary heritage.

## 5. Hangzhou Attractions and Activities

### West Lake Explorations

Hangzhou's crown gem, West Lake, has a lot to offer in terms of sights to see and things to do.

Take a boat trip on West Water to explore the many islands and enjoy the tranquility of the water.

**Cycling Around the Lake:** For beautiful vistas, rent a bicycle and ride the well-paved routes.

**Leifeng Pagoda**: Climb this ancient pagoda to see sweeping views of West Lake and learn about its storied history.

**The Hangzhou Botanical Garden** is a great place to take a leisurely walk amid a variety of plant types. It is located close to West Lake.

### Historic Sites

Hangzhou's well-preserved landmarks are rich in historical reflections.

**Lingyin Temple**: With its elaborate sculptures and serene atmosphere, this old Buddhist temple is tucked away in the hills.

**Six Harmonies Pagoda:** This architectural wonder is perched atop Yuelun Hill with a view of the Qiantang River.

**Former Hu Xueyan Residence:** Tour this opulent mansion from the 19th century that has traditional Chinese architecture and was owned by a well-known businessman.

## Galleries and Museums

Hangzhou's museums and galleries are veritable gold mines for culture and art lovers.

- Zhejiang Provincial Museum: With its extensive collection of antiquities, this museum offers insights into the history and culture of the region.
- Explore the history of silk manufacturing and its significance in Hangzhou by visiting the China National Silk Museum.
- Modern creative expressions may be shown in the Contemporary Art Museum in Hangzhou, a center for contemporary art.

Participating in these events guarantees a wonderful tourist experience by delving deeply into Hangzhou's cultural, historical, and artistic aspects.

## Gardens & Parks

Some of China's most exquisite parks and gardens may be found in Hangzhou, providing peaceful escapes and breathtaking scenery.

- Discover this verdant and tranquil wetland ecosystem in Xixi National Wetland Park by boat or on foot.
- Quyuan Park: Known for its lotus blossoms, this park is a great place to unwind and take pictures of the natural world.
- Taiziwan Park is a great place for picnics and is adorned with cherry blossoms in the spring. It is situated on the west side of West Lake.

## Shopping Districts

Hangzhou offers a range of shopping experiences, from contemporary malls to traditional marketplaces.

- Hangzhou Tower Shopping City: An upscale retail location with an array of premium brands.
- Wulin Square: Department shops and fashion boutiques may be found in the square's immediate vicinity.

- Hefang Street: An old street with tourist shops, tea, silk, and traditional Chinese crafts.

## Day Trips from Hangzhou

Many places in the vicinity of Hangzhou are excellent for day visits.

> ➤ Wuzhen Water Town is a historical town with canals, historic buildings, and a rich cultural legacy that has been wonderfully maintained.
>
> ➤ Take pleasure in sailing, fishing, and island exploration at Thousand Islets Lake (Qiandao Lake).
>
> ➤ The lush green bamboo forest in Anji gives a unique experience and is wonderful for trekking and taking in the serene surroundings.

Visitors may take in the natural, cultural, and regional richness of Hangzhou and its environs by visiting these locations.

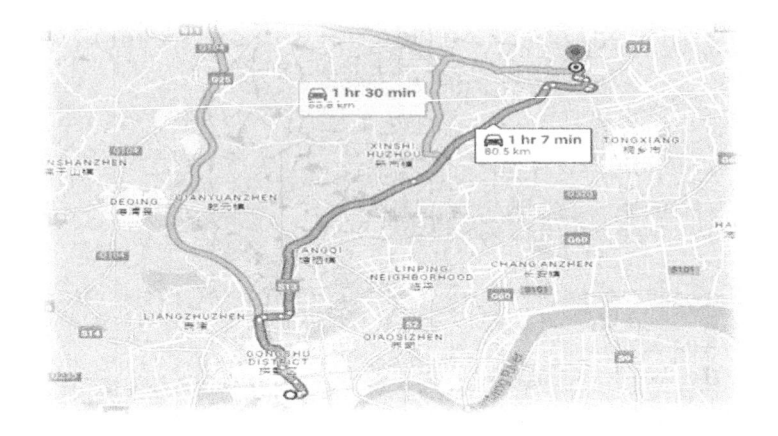

*Wuzhen Water Town*

## 6. Culture and Festival

Hangzhou, with its profound history and cultural heritage, is a city that weaves traditional festivals and contemporary events into the fabric of everyday life. Here's an overview that could be a section in a travel guide:

## Traditional Festivals

### Spring Festival (Chinese New Year):

The most important celebration in Chinese culture, with Hangzhou offering temple fairs, dragon dances, and special culinary feasts.

### Qingming Festival (Tomb-Sweeping Day):

An occasion for paying respect to ancestors, it's also a time when Hangzhou's natural beauty is in full bloom, and outdoor activities are abundant.

### Dragon Boat Festival:

Witness the excitement of dragon boat races on the West Lake and partake in eating zongzi (sticky rice dumplings wrapped in bamboo leaves).

### Mid-Autumn Festival:

Families gather to enjoy mooncakes and admire the full moon, with lantern displays and poetry readings by the West Lake.

**Double Ninth Festival:**

Known as Chongyang, this festival involves climbing mountains and appreciating chrysanthemum flowers, a tradition that is alive and well in Hangzhou's numerous parks and green spaces.

## Contemporary Cultural Events

**West Lake Expo:**

An annual event that showcases technological advancements, art, and cultural exchanges.

**Hangzhou International Film Festival:**

A platform for global cinema with a special focus on Asian filmmakers, accompanied by workshops and director talks.

**Hangzhou Animation Festival:**

A celebration of the animation industry, featuring screenings, exhibitions, and a cosplay carnival.

## Performing Arts

Impression West Lake:

A nightly outdoor performance directed by renowned director Zhang Yimou, blending music, light, and dance to narrate local legends.

Hangzhou Opera:

Experience traditional Chinese opera with a Hangzhou twist, known for its elegant performances and distinctive local flair.

Live Music and Theatre:

Hangzhou's modern venues and traditional stages host a variety of live performances ranging from classical music concerts to contemporary theatre productions.

## Tea Culture

Longjing Tea Plantation Visits:

Explore the plantations where the world-famous Longjing (Dragon Well) tea is grown, and learn about the delicate art of tea picking and roasting.

**China National Tea Museum**:

Delve into the history of Chinese tea culture, participate in tea tastings, and attend workshops on tea preparation and appreciation.

**Tea Ceremonies:**

Participate in a traditional Chinese tea ceremony, a meditative practice that has been perfected over centuries.

**Tea Festivals:**

Join in on the celebrations during the annual tea harvest season, with events that include tea picking experiences and market fairs where you can buy the freshest Longjing tea.

Incorporating these cultural elements provides a rich tapestry of experiences for visitors, allowing them to engage with the ancient traditions and modern vibes of Hangzhou. Whether it's through the solemnity of traditional observances or the vibrancy of contemporary festivals, Hangzhou offers a unique glimpse into the cultural heart of China.

# MY travel Experience

# 7. Useful Travelers Information

## Health and Safety

With a low crime rate, Hangzhou is a usually safe city for visitors. Nonetheless, common sense measures must be followed:

**Personal Safety**: Be mindful of your surroundings, particularly in busy areas, and keep your valuables safe.

**Health:** Bottled water is readily accessible, however, tap water is not fit for human consumption. Pharmacies are widespread and have some employees who know English, and hospitals are well-equipped.

**Travel Insurance:** Since medical treatment for foreign nationals may be costly, it is important to carry travel insurance that includes health coverage.

**Emergency Phone Numbers:** 110 for law enforcement, 120 for emergency medical assistance, and 119 for firefighters.

## Money and Tipping

The yuan (¥) is the fundamental unit of currency in China, which is the Renminbi (RMB).

**Currency exchange:** Banks, hotels, and airports provide it. Most ATMs accept foreign cards and are commonly available.

**Credit Cards:** Hotels, large eateries, and retail establishments accept major credit cards. Smaller sellers, meanwhile, could only take cash or purchases made via mobile apps like Alipay or WeChat Pay.

**Tipping**: In China, leaving a gratuity is neither customary nor anticipated. Nonetheless, tipping regulations may apply to upscale eateries and lodging facilities that host guests from abroad.

Knowing these useful details will help to guarantee a hassle-free and pleasurable trip to Hangzhou.

## Language and Communication

In Hangzhou, Mandarin Chinese is the official language. Since English is not frequently spoken, the following advice is provided:

- ➤ Language applications: To assist with basic conversation, bring a phrasebook or use translation applications on your phone.
- ➤ Mandarin Phrases: It might be quite beneficial to learn a few essential Mandarin phrases for transactions, instructions, and greetings.
- ➤ Business Cards: Have one side of your business card printed with your information in Chinese if you are here on business.

## Cultural Etiquettes

It will improve your experience and demonstrate respect for the culture if you are aware of local practices.

In greetings, it's customary to nod or bow slightly. Although you should wait for your Chinese colleague to begin, handshakes are also appropriate.

Face (Mianzi): Keep your dignity intact; Chinese culture values neither humiliation nor conflict.

Present Giving: It's customary to bring a modest present when you're welcomed to someone's house. Clocks, sharp things, and the number four should be avoided since they are connected to death and misfortune.

## Packing Checklist

Think about including the following goods on your packing list for your trip to Hangzhou:

- ➢ Dress appropriately for the weather, bringing layers for fluctuating temperatures and rain gear for the rainy season.
- ➢ Comfy Shoes: Whether strolling through parks, the city, or West Lake.
- ➢ Electrical Adapters: Because China utilizes 220V electricity, be sure your equipment has the appropriate adapters.
- ➢ Personal Medications: Please provide a copy of your prescriptions as well as the generic names, as some brands may not be accessible.

- Pollution Mask: You may need one if you're going at a time when pollution levels are high.
- Travel Documents: Chinese hotel/address information, passport, visa, and travel insurance.

Planning a polite and hassle-free trip to Hangzhou should be made easier with the aid of our checklist and cultural etiquette tips

# MY travel Experience

## 8. Itineraries and Guided Tours

**Hangzhou in a Day:**

If you just have a little time, concentrate on the must-see sights.

- Morning: Take a stroll around West Lake in the morning before going to the Lingyin Temple.
- Afternoon: Visit the China National Silk Museum or the China National Tea Museum after eating lunch at a neighborhood eatery by the lake.
- Evening: Take a stroll down Hefang Street for supper and shopping, taking in the lively nightlife.

Three-Day High Points:

An extended visit enables a deeper exploration.

- Day 1: Spend the day exploring West Lake, which includes a boat trip, the Leifeng Pagoda, and the Broken Bridge. To see the lotus blossoms, go to Quyuan Gardens.
- Day 2: Visit historical locations such as Six Harmonies Pagoda and Lingyin Temple. Take in an

impressionist show in the evening, like "Impression West Lake".
> Day 3: Enjoy a leisurely day in Xixi National Wetland Park or go to one of the neighboring water towns, like as Wuzhen or Xitang.

**Themed Tours**

Themed tours may make the trip more enjoyable for those with particular interests.

- Cultural Tour: To learn about Hangzhou's past and culture, concentrate on visiting historical places and museums.
- Gastronomy trip: Take a culinary trip to explore the regional cuisine, which includes fine dining, street food, and tea culture.
- Nature and Adventure Tour: Arrange outdoor activities such as riding around West Lake, hiking in the nearby hills, or exploring the wetlands.

Although these itineraries provide organized alternatives, they may be altered to suit individual preferences and travel styles.

## Off-the-Beaten-Path

Discovering Hangzhou outside of the typical tourist traps might result in interesting and unforgettable encounters. Here are some suggestions for exploring less traveled paths:

**Meijiawu Tea Village:** Nestled among the verdant hills of Hangzhou's tea farms, Meijiawu is a great spot to experience a traditional tea ceremony away from the throng and learn about Chinese tea culture.

**Sleeping of the Tiger Spring:** Although West Lake is the main draw, this lesser-known spring is a peaceful location with a fable that the water was formed by a tiger that was sleeping.

**Yangmeiling town:** Tucked up in the mountains, this little town is ideal for anyone looking for a tranquil getaway and a taste of rural Hangzhou life.

**Nine Creeks Winding** Through a Misty Forest (Jiuxi 18 Stream): Take a walk beside the streams and indulge in the unspoiled natural splendor of the region, which is particularly lovely in the fall foliage or during the spring blossoming season.

**Former Hu Xueyan Residence**: Explore this exquisitely restored Qing Dynasty palace with elaborate architecture and an intriguing history, owned by one of China's most successful businesspeople.

**Hangzhou Botanical Garden**: Although many visitors focus on the city's well-known parks, the botanical garden offers a lovely, serene setting for admiring a wide range of plants and flowers.

**Xiang Lake (Xianghu): With** a somewhat calmer atmosphere than West Lake, Xiang Lake is great for strolls, picnics, and taking in the tranquil views of the lake.

**Experience the Grand Canal by boat**, the world's oldest and longest waterway, where you can view historic bridges and get a taste of life along the banks.

Explore these lesser-known areas of Hangzhou to experience a calm and authentic side of the city that many tourists overlook.

# APPENDICES

## Information about Visas

Typically, visitors to Hangzhou need a Chinese visa, which may be obtained ahead of time from the Chinese consulate or embassy in their home nation. Depending on the traveler's nationality and intent, different criteria apply. Some things to think about are:

- Tourist visas, often known as L visas, are typically good for 30 to 90 days.

- Visa Exemptions: If a person meets specific requirements, such as having a transit visa that lasts 72 or 144 hours, they may be able to enter the country for a brief period without a visa.

- Documentation: Make sure you have all the essential paperwork, such as evidence of return or forward travel and, if needed, an invitation letter.

## Handy Apps & Websites

The following websites and applications may come in handy while you're there:

- WeChat/Weixin: For mobile payments, communication, and more uses.
- Alipay is a popular mobile payment app.
- China's dependable mapping provider is Baidu Maps.
- China Train Ticketing: For train timetables and reservations.
- Didi Chuxing is the Chinese version of Uber for private vehicles and taxis.
- Pleco: An OCR-enabled English-Chinese dictionary app that can read menus and signage.
- CTrip: For making domestic travel, hotel, and rail reservations in China.

## Emergency Numbers:

Having a list of emergency contacts is essential:

- 110 Local Police
- 120 ambulances
- Department of Fire: 119
- 122 traffic accidents
- Local Embassy or Consulate: Contact information for the diplomatic mission of your nation in China.
- For the most up-to-date information, always consult official sources before departing.

# My travel Experience

# Calendar of Events for the Year

**January**

New Year's Eve celebrations include street parties, light displays, and fireworks across the whole city.

Hangzhou Tea Culture Festival: A week-long celebration with tea tastings and cultural events honoring Hangzhou's tea legacy.

**February**

Lantern Festival: Traditional activities and meals are served under colorful lanterns that beautify the city, particularly near West Lake.

Spring Festival: Dragon dances, temple festivals, and other unique festivities mark the start of the Chinese New Year.

**March**

Qingming Festival: Also referred to as Tomb-Sweeping Day, this occasion is used to pay tribute to ancestors via a variety of traditional practices.

## April

West Lake International Expo: Featuring displays of regional artwork, crafts, and culture.

The Hangzhou Asian Cuisine Festival is an event that brings together chefs and food sellers to showcase the finest Asian culinary customs.

## May

Highlights of the Dragon Boat Festival include the traditional zongzi (rice dumplings) and the dragon boat races on West Lake.

International Tea Festival: Ceremonies and tastings honoring Hangzhou's renowned Longjing tea.

## June

Hangzhou Cultural and Creative Industry Expo: Locally handcrafted goods on display and for sale.

Midsummer Carnival: An event showcasing both domestic and foreign musicians and visual artists.

## July

Lotus Festival: Cultural activities and photographic competitions coincide with the blooming of West Lake's lotus blossoms.

Hangzhou Silk Fashion Week: Silk, a regional specialty, is the centerpiece of fashion shows and exhibitions.

## August

Known as Chinese Valentine's Day, the Qixi Festival has amorous festivities all around the city.

The Hangzhou International Animation Festival offers animation aficionados conferences, workshops, and screenings.

## September

Mid-Autumn Festival: Mooncake baking, puzzles with lanterns, and get-togethers with family to see the full moon.

Chinese arts and crafts, both traditional and contemporary, are on display at the Hangzhou Arts and Crafts Fair.

## October

National Day Golden Week is a week of events honoring the People's Republic of China's establishment.

Hangzhou International Music Festival: Classical, traditional, and modern music performed in concerts.

## November

One of the biggest animation festivals in China, the China International Cartoon & Animation Festival includes trade seminars, conferences, and exhibits.

Hangzhou Citizens' Tourism Festival: Promotion of local tourism via events and deals at popular tourist destinations.

## December

Christmas markets have grown in popularity even though they are not a traditional Chinese festival.

The annual Hangzhou Marathon draws participants from all around the globe.

# MY travel Experience

# My travel Experience

# Bonus Chapters

## Phrasebook Guide

Here are 20 helpful Mandarin Chinese phrases with their pronunciation guides for an English speaker visiting Hangzhou:

| |
|---|
| Hello: 你好 (Nǐ hǎo) – Nee how |
| Thank you: 谢谢 (Xièxiè) – Shyeah-shyeah |
| Yes: 是 (Shì) – Shrr |
| No: 不是 (Bù shì) – Boo shrr |
| Please: 请 (Qǐng) – Ching |
| Excuse me/Sorry: 对不起 (Duìbuqǐ) – Dway-boo-chee |
| I don't understand: 我不懂 (Wǒ bù dǒng) – Woh boo dong |
| Where is the bathroom?: 洗手间在哪里? (Xǐshǒujiān zài nǎlǐ?) – Shee-shoh-jee-an zeye na-lee? |
| How much is this?: 这个多少钱? (Zhège duōshǎo qián?) – Juh-guh dwor-shao chyen? |

Can you help me?: 你能帮我吗? (Nǐ néng bāng wǒ ma?) – Nee nung bung woh ma?

I'm looking for...: 我找... (Wǒ zhǎo...) – Woh jow...

I would like to order...: 我想点... (Wǒ xiǎng diǎn...) – Woh shee-ang dee-an...

Do you speak English?: 你会说英语吗? (Nǐ huì shuō Yīngyǔ ma?) – Nee hway shwo Ying-yoo ma?

I'm allergic to...: 我对...过敏 (Wǒ duì... guòmǐn) – Woh dway... gwor-meen

Water, please: 请给我水 (Qǐng gěi wǒ shuǐ) – Ching gay woh shway

This is too expensive: 这个太贵了 (Zhège tài guìle) – Juh-guh tie gway luh

Where can I find a taxi?: 我在哪里可以找到出租车? (Wǒ zài nǎlǐ kěyǐ zhǎodào chūzūchē?) – Woh zeye na-lee kuh-ee jow-dow choo-zoo-chuh?

I need a doctor: 我需要医生 (Wǒ xūyào yīshēng) – Woh shoo-yow ee-shung

| |
|---|
| Cheers!: 干杯! (Gānbēi!) – Gan-bay! |
| Goodbye: 再见 (Zàijiàn) – Zeye-jee-an |

These phrases cover basic interactions and can be quite helpful for navigating day-to-day situations in Hangzhou.

## Sample Itineraries
### Family-Friendly Adventure Itinerary

**Day 1: West Lake and Hangzhou Zoo**

- Start your day with a leisurely boat ride on West Lake.
- Visit the nearby Hangzhou Botanical Garden for a picnic.
- Spend the afternoon at Hangzhou Zoo to see the pandas.

### Day 2: Songcheng Park

- Enjoy the amusement rides and live performances at Songcheng Park.
- Have lunch at the park's restaurant, offering local dishes.
- Visit the Song Dynasty Town, a theme park bringing ancient China to life.

### Day 3: Xixi National Wetland Park

- Explore the Xixi National Wetland Park with a guided boat tour.
- Participate in interactive cultural activities like traditional fishing or silk painting.
- End your day with a meal at a family-friendly restaurant serving Hangzhou cuisine.

## Solo Travelers Itinerary

### Day 1: Lingyin Temple and Feilai Peak

- Start with a morning hike to Feilai Peak to see ancient Buddhist carvings.
- Explore the peaceful grounds of Lingyin Temple.

Dine at a local café and enjoy some quiet reflection or reading.

## Day 2: Museums and Teahouses

- o  Visit the China National Tea Museum and the China National Silk Museum.
- o  Spend the afternoon in a traditional teahouse, perhaps engaging with locals or other travelers.
- o  Explore the shopping districts and local markets.

## Day 3: Hike and Hot Springs

- o  Hike the trails of the bamboo-lined path at Moganshan.
- o  Relax in the evening at a local hot spring resort.

## Romantic Adventure Itinerary

### Day 1: West Lake and Surrounds

- o  Begin with a private boat tour of West Lake at sunrise.
- o  Stroll hand-in-hand along the Su Causeway.
- o  Have a romantic dinner at a lakeside restaurant.

## Day 2: Wine and Tea

- Visit the Chateau Moutai for wine tasting.
- Walk through the Meijiawu Tea Village and partake in a tea ceremony.
- End your day with a sunset view from the city's pagodas.

## Day 3: Nature and Serenity

- Visit the secluded Nine Creeks in a Misty Forest for a peaceful walk.
- Enjoy a couples' spa day at a luxury resort.

### Culinary Adventure Itinerary
## Day 1: Local Markets and Street Food

- Visit the Wushan Square Street Market to try various local snacks.
- Take a cooking class focused on Hangzhou cuisine.
- Explore the night market for more culinary delights.

## Day 2: Tea Culture and Fine Dining

- Spend the morning at Longjing Village to learn about Dragon Well tea.
- Have lunch at a restaurant known for its Beggar's Chicken, a Hangzhou specialty.
- Dine at a Michelin-starred restaurant for an upscale take on local dishes.

**Day 3: Food Tour and Brewery Visit**

- Join a guided food tour to taste various local dishes and learn about their history.
- Visit a local craft brewery to taste Chinese-style craft beers.
- End your trip with a dinner cruise on West Lake, enjoying Hangzhou's flavors as you take in the night scenery.

# MY travel Experience

# Hangzhou Restaurant Guide with Local Recipes

## 1. Lou Wai Lou (楼外楼)

Location: No. 30 Gushan Road, Xihu District, Hangzhou

**Must-Try Dish: West Lake Fish in Vinegar Gravy**

Recipe Overview: A traditional Hangzhou dish where a fresh grass carp from West Lake is poached and served with a sweet and sour sauce made from vinegar and sugar.

Ordering Tip: This dish is best enjoyed fresh; ask for the mildest version if you're not accustomed to strong flavors.

## 2. Grandma's Home (外婆家)

Location: Multiple locations across Hangzhou

**Must-Try Dish: Dongpo Pork**

Recipe Overview: This is a slow-cooked pork belly dish, braised in bamboo leaves, Shaoxing wine, and soy sauce until tender.

Ordering Tip: Pair it with a local green tea to balance the richness of the meat.

## 3. Zhi Wei Guan (知味观)

Location: 83 Renhe Road, Shangcheng District, Hangzhou

**Must-Try Dish: Beggar's Chicken**

Recipe Overview: The chicken is marinated, stuffed with mushrooms and spices, wrapped in lotus leaves, encased in clay, and roasted for hours.

Ordering Tip: Order in advance as this dish takes a long time to prepare.

## 4. Hangzhou Snack Street

Location: Hefang Street, Shangcheng District, Hangzhou

**Must-Try Dish: Xiaolongbao (Soup Dumplings)**

Recipe Overview: Thin dumpling skins are filled with a mixture of meat and gelatin-rich broth that melts into soup when steamed.

Ordering Tip: Be careful when biting into these as the soup inside can be hot.

## 5. Green Tea Restaurant (绿茶餐厅)

Location: No. 83 Longjing Road, Xihu District, Hangzhou

**Must-Try Dish: Longjing Shrimp**

Recipe Overview: This dish features river shrimp cooked with Longjing tea leaves, showcasing a delicate tea fragrance.

Ordering Tip: It's a delicate dish, so it's best not to pair it with strong flavors.

## 6. 28 Hubin Road

Location: Hyatt Regency Hangzhou, 28 Hubin Road, Hangzhou

**Must-Try Dish: Hangzhou Pepper Duck**

Recipe Overview: Duck marinated with Sichuan peppers and other spices, roasted to achieve a crispy skin and tender meat.

Ordering Tip: This dish may be spicier than typical Hangzhou cuisine, so indicate your spice preference when ordering.

**For an Immersive Experience:**

- Photography: Collaborate with local photographers or restaurants to feature high-quality images of the dishes.
- Recipes: Partner with chefs to create step-by-step recipe cards or booklets that visitors can take home.
- Local Insights: Include quotes from local food critics or chefs about what makes each dish special.
- Cultural Context: Provide background on the historical and cultural significance of each dish.

Remember, the best restaurant guides not only suggest where to eat but also help diners understand and appreciate the local food culture.

# Hangzhou Shopping Guide for Visitors

## 1. Hangzhou Silk City (杭州丝绸城)

Location: 253 Xinhua Road, Xiacheng District, Hangzhou

Opening Hours: 8:30 am – 6:30 pm

What to Find: An array of silk products including scarves, clothing, bedding, and accessories. Known for its quality silk and a wide range of prices.

Popular Items: Silk scarves and qipao dresses.

Insider Tip: Bargaining is expected; start at about 40% of the asking price and settle for around 60%.

## 2. Hefang Street (河坊街)

Location: Shangcheng District, Hangzhou

Opening Hours: 9:00 am – 10:00 pm

What to Find: A historic street with a variety of shops selling traditional Chinese medicine, tea, souvenirs, and snacks.

Popular Items: Longjing tea, traditional snacks like dragon-whisker candy.

Insider Tip: Visit in the evening when the street comes alive with performers and traditional games.

### 3. Wushan Night Market (吴山夜市)

Location: On Wushan Hill, near Hefang Street, Hangzhou

Opening Hours: 6:00 pm – 10:00 pm

What to Find: Stalls selling crafts, souvenirs, and clothing at budget prices.

Popular Items: Handicrafts, fans, and beaded jewelry.

Insider Tip: The market is only open in the evenings, so plan your visit accordingly.

## 4. Hangzhou Tower Shopping Mall (杭州大厦购物城)

Location: 1 Wulin Square, Xiacheng District, Hangzhou

Opening Hours: 10:00 am – 10:00 pm

What to Find: A modern shopping center with international brands, luxury goods, and fine dining options.

Popular Items: Designer clothing and accessories.

Insider Tip: Check out the top floor for gourmet restaurants and a great view of the city.

## 5. The MixC Mall (万象城)

Location: 701 Fuchun Road, Jianggan District, Hangzhou

Opening Hours: 10:00 am – 10:00 pm

What to Find: High-end shopping with a mix of international and domestic brands, electronics, and a large food court.

Popular Items: Electronics and brand-name fashion.

Insider Tip: The basement food court offers a variety of local Hangzhou cuisine.

## 6. Qinghefang Ancient Street (清河坊古街)

Location: Near Wushan Square, Hangzhou

Opening Hours: 9:00 am – 10:00 pm

What to Find: Traditional and cultural goods, antiques, and Chinese art.

Popular Items: Porcelain, calligraphy, and paintings.

Insider Tip: Visit the traditional Chinese medicine shops to see a piece of living history.

## 7. Intime Mall (银泰百货)

Location: Multiple locations across Hangzhou

Opening Hours: 10:00 am – 10:00 pm

What to Find: A mix of shopping, entertainment, and dining with a focus on mid-range to high-end products.

Popular Items: Cosmetics and fashion wear.

Insider Tip: Look out for seasonal sales, especially during Chinese festivals, for substantial discounts.

## Shopping Tips for Visitors

Bargaining: Always polite and with a smile. In malls, prices are fixed, but in markets, you should negotiate.

Quality: Check the quality of the products, especially if they are branded items, to ensure authenticity.

Payment: While many places accept credit cards, having some cash is useful, especially in markets.

Language: Having a translation app or a phrasebook can be handy when shopping in local markets.

This guide should serve as a starting point for visitors looking to explore Hangzhou's shopping scene, with the potential to be expanded with more details and updated information as needed.

# My travel Experience

_____

_____

_____

_____

_____

_____

_____

_____

_____

_____

_____

_____

_____

Printed in Great Britain
by Amazon